Moss Moments
Exploring the World's Most Enchanting Forests

Table of Contents

Chapter 1. Introduction

Welcome, nature lovers and curious explorers, to 'Moss Moments: Exploring the World's Most Enchanting Forests', our meticulously crafted Special Report that invites you on a voyage into nature's verdant realm. Here, you don't just read, you experience. Marvel at the exquisite photographic illustrations of moss-shrouded woods worldwide, feel the hum of life in every bough, trunk, and leaf, and uncover the mystifying stories of flora and fauna that have captivated imaginations for generations. Whether a seasoned botanist, a dedicated conservationist, or just a humble individual seeking solace in the emerald embrace of nature, you'll discover worlds primeval yet untouched, dense, and full of wonder. Come, let's dive deep into this mossy labyrinth—it's an exploration you won't want to miss, so why not secure your copy today and start your adventure? Let the enchanting forests of the world unfurl before your eyes with every turn of the page in this mesmerizing Special Report!

Chapter 2. The Green Carpet: An Introduction to Moss

To tread on a rich, plush carpet of moss is like stepping back in time, immersing oneself in a world both ancient and incredibly intricate.

2.1. Origins Rooted in Deep Time

Centuries old, moss has been a part of our planet's flora since the first days of terrestrial life. Believe it or not, these humble plants have been weaving their emerald tapestry for over 470 million years. The first land-dwelling plants, the progenitors of today's mosses, were quite unlike what we're used to seeing today. They did not have roots, no flowers nor seeds, and not a single leaf to their name. Instead, they were a primitive assembly of tissues, a precursor to the complex microscopic structures that mosses have developed today.

Different in form, yes, but their purpose and functionality was as colossal as it is now. Since then, mosses have played a crucial role in shaping the environment as we know it. By pioneering colonization of raw, harsh landscapes and initiating soil production, they have made Earth viable for future, more complex forms of plant life.

2.2. Classification and Varieties

There are approximately 12,000 different species of moss classified into three distinct types: acrocarps, pleurocarps, and sphagnums, each with its unique characteristics and adaptations.

Acrocarps grow upright, resembling tiny trees. Pleurocarps, on the other hand, grow horizontally and form a dense mat on the substrate. The sphagnums, also known as peat mosses, possess a unique structure enabling their use in various applications such as potting mix and wound dressing due to their absorbent nature.

2.3. Moss Anatomy and Adaptations

The structure of moss is as unique as its history. Unlike the more familiar trees, flowers, and grasses that are vascular plants, mosses are non-vascular. They lack roots, leaves, and a stem in the true sense. Instead, they possess a fascinating physiological framework including rhizoids, stems, and leaves. Moreover, the absence of vascular tissues leads to some exceptional adaptations like the ability to survive in inhospitable environments.

Each moss plant begins its life as a small spore, eventually maturing into a sporophyte which produces more spores, repeating the cycle of life. Given the right conditions – shade, bare soil, and enough moisture – mosses can establish themselves quickly, creating verdant mosaics in forests, lawns, and even in the corners of your backyard garden.

2.4. Moss in Ecosystem: the Underestimated Powerhouse

Mosses play a more significant role in ecosystems than most give them credit for. They aid in maintaining the moisture level in forests, playing an essential role in the water economy. By holding onto rainwater, they help to control erosion and provide a lush carpet that serves as a home for insects, spiders, and other small creatures.

They aren't just good at preserving water; mosses also excel at capturing nutrients. They capture airborne nutrients from both rain and dust and release these into the surrounding ecosystem. When mosses die, they give back their stored nutrients, further enriching the soil.

In the colder regions of the world, mosses insulate the ground, protecting the root systems of larger plants. They also have a symbiotic relationship with trees, growing on weak branches, providing nutrients, and aiding in decomposition once the branch falls.

2.5. Decoding Moss Colors

While green is the color most associated with moss, they do come in a variety of colors, including red, orange, yellow, blue, and even black. Color can often be an indicator of the moss's condition. A moss that has turned brown, for example, may be too dry or suffering from pollution.

2.6. Moss: Humans' Ancient Aid and Modern Use

Moss's utility to humans is as expansive as their varieties. They've been traditionally used for many purposes — as filling for mattresses and pillows, being part of the structural framework of homes, and even as an early form of antiseptic dressing for wounds during the World Wars.

Today, mosses are recognized for a wide range of applications, from bioindication (indicating air quality and pollution levels), urban greening, to creating art in the form of intricate, maintenance-free moss walls and panels.

2.7. The Future of Mosses

Finally, as we get ready to step into the future, mosses are showing no signs of slowing down. Scientists are now testing them as potential biofuels. With their ability to absorb copious amounts of CO_2, they are also on track to become front-line soldiers in the fight against climate change.

We have just scratched the surface of understanding these fascinating entities. So, let us continue to explore, to admire, and yes, even to tread softly on that lush, green carpet beneath our feet, for it has stories to tell, functions to perform, and countless wonders to add to our world.

Chapter 3. The Secrets of Photosynthesis: Moss in Action

In the deep corners of the world's enchanting forests lies a humble yet paramount component of our ecosystem—the moss. This verdant carpet that oftentimes goes unnoticed is more complex than meets the eye; it plays an essential role in our world via an intricate process known as photosynthesis.

3.1. The Intricacies of Photosynthesis in Moss

Photosynthesis, the process through which light energy is converted into chemical energy, is the veritable lifeblood, not just of moss but of all photosynthetic organisms on earth. In moss however, this process takes somewhat of a unique turn. Unlike higher plants, mosses do not have a deep root system for water and nutrient absorption. They gather the majority of required elements, including water, directly from precipitation and air through their leaves.

While sunshine is a critical component for photosynthesis in most plants, mosses have evolved to tolerate low light conditions. Found in the dappled shade beneath towering redwoods or clinging to the shadowy sides of rocks and trees, they have a beautifully complex system that allows them to photosynthesize efficiently in these sub-optimal conditions.

3.2. Factors Affecting Photosynthesis in Moss

Multiple factors impact moss's photosynthetic process. Light intensity, water availability, and carbon dioxide levels are among the crucial influencers. Mosses have the fascinating ability to swiftly suspend their metabolic processes during desiccation and resume them shortly after they receive water. This attribute is a product of moss modulation of photosynthetic machinery according to hydration and dehydration cycles, earning it the moniker of "resurrection plant".

An increase in carbon dioxide levels also significantly boosts moss's photosynthetic rate. The mechanism allows more substantial carbon removal from the atmosphere than we previously understood, marking mosses as unsung heroes in the global carbon cycle and potential allies combating climate change.

3.3. The Magic of Chloroplasts in Moss Cells

At the heart of moss's photosynthesis lies the chloroplast, the cellular organelle where this magic unfolds. Moss cells may contain several small chloroplasts as compared to the single large chloroplast found in higher plants.

Moss chloroplasts also exhibit a remarkable characteristic—they can move! Depending on the light intensity, these chloroplasts can shift en masse deeper into the cell during high light intensities to prevent photodamage. Conversely, in low light conditions, they accumulate just beneath the cell surface to optimize light absorption. This feature underscores the adaptability of mosses to their changing environment.

3.4. The Path of Carbon through Mosses

As mosses lack typical leaf stomata, they possess distinctive gas exchange pathways for carbon. In a process comparable to vascular plants, carbon dioxide diffuses into the leaf and encounters the enzyme Rubisco, facilitating its conversion to carbohydrate through the Calvin-Benson cycle. This cycle forms the basis of carbon fixation in mosses. The carbohydrates produced here will give the moss the energy it requires to grow and reproduce, simultaneously releasing oxygen into the atmosphere.

Yet, the path doesn't end there; some carbon will be channeled into the moss's broader ecosystem through an array of interactions with microbes and fauna, while a larger portion will be locked into the dense moss mat.

3.5. Moss: An Underestimated Player in the Global Carbon Cycle

Often dismissed due to their small size, mosses have been underestimated players in the global carbon cycle. They sequester a significant amount of carbon per day, much more than that absorbed by a similar area of forest.

Moss-rich ecosystems such as boreal peatlands store up to one-third of global terrestrial carbon, much of it millennia-old, subsequently preventing its release into the atmosphere. This long-term carbon store demonstrates the truly significant role that moss plays not only concerning photosynthesis but also in influencing global carbon fluxes and potentially climate change trajectories.

Thus, the journey of moss is truly an intricate dance of elements and energy. From the smallest chlorophyll-filled chloroplasts to the vast global carbon stores, the photosynthetic journey of moss elucidates the interconnectedness of our natural world and underscores the importance of these verdant, mossy worlds beneath our feet.

In the end, the journey of moss from sunshine to complex organic matter is a testament to Earth's incredible, verdant life systems. Through this intricate pathway, delicate and resilient moss serves as a powerful reminder of how even the smallest, most overlooked beings play significant roles in our planet's broader life-sustaining processes. As such, we should afford them the appreciation they so rightfully deserve. There is indeed much to be learned from taking a moment to explore the miniature, mossy worlds at our feet.

Chapter 4. Legends and Lore: Moss in Cultural Context

Legend has it, the first spore of moss that sprouted on ancient Earth was a harbinger of the green explosion that eventually breathed life into the stark granite topography. Indeed, these tiny organisms have pervaded our planet's greener spaces and our cultural context for aeons.

4.1. Moss in Mythology and Folklore

Moss has played a significant role in both Eastern and Western folklore. In European myths, it is often considered a symbol of humility due to its ability to thrive even in the harshest of environments. One of the most famous moss-related folklore stories is that of the "moss maiden" or "wood woman," characters found in the folk tales of Germany's Black Forest. These enchanting beings, often shown adorned with mossy garments, were believed to be forest spirits, protectors of woodlands and all their inhabitants.

Across the pond, Native American tribes also held moss in high regard. They believed that moss, unlike other vegetation, was a nocturnal plant. According to their lore, moss was thought to grow only in moonlight, weaving its magic in sync with the rhythm of the moon's cycles. It was a symbol of balance, resilience, and endurance.

In Eastern culture, too, moss is deeply revered. Japanese gardens often cultivate moss due to its embodiment of tranquility, peace, and age. In Shinto beliefs, moss is both a decorative and a spiritual element, an emblem of harmony and patience.

4.2. Moss and Magic: A Peek into the Occult

In the world of the occult and magic, moss has a fascinating space where its subtle energy is utilized for healing, protection, and manifestation of wealth. In Celtic traditions, moss-amulets were made, revered for their purported power to bring fortune or even to ward off evil spirits.

Druids, a religious order in ancient British and Gaulish societies, considered oaks festooned with moss to be sacred. Kingly groves, as they were often denoted, were revered places for worship, believed to attract fairies and other supernatural beings.

Of course, one can't ignore the lore of luck attributed to the Irish moss, Carrageen. It's said that carrying a bit of this sea moss will attract luck and prosperity—a belief still quite prevalent, especially during St. Patrick's Day celebrations.

4.3. Moss in Literature and Art

The prevalence of moss isn't limited to myths and old wives' tales; it has also made considerable appearances in literature and art. From Romantic-era poets who were captivated by the hauntingly beautiful aesthetics of moss-covered landscapes, to contemporary writers who find solace and inspiration in these small-scaled forms of greenery, moss has effortlessly landed on paper.

British author Elizabeth Gaskell, for instance, explored moss symbolism in her novel, 'Cranford', where moss represents the possibility for growth and change.

In visual arts, too, the presence of moss is a motif that conveys the passage of time, the permanence of nature, and the essence of life. It can be seen in the works of famed artists such as Claude Monet and

Caspar David Friedrich, adding texture, depth, and subtle vitality to their masterpieces.

4.4. Moss: The Cultural Catalyst

Gradually, moss's cultural invasion has touched modern, urban landscapes as well. The trend of 'moss graffiti'— a form of eco-art using moss blended with other materials to create an organic, living paint that can grow on walls and other surfaces—reflects a union between art, nature, and activism.

Global societies today are revisiting the wisdom in old folklore, recognizing the profound understanding our ancestors had of their coexistence with nature, where moss played an integral role.

4.5. Conclusion: Moss, A Tapestry Weaved Over Time

Despite its often-overlooked presence in the natural world, moss's cultural resonance is deeply woven into our societal fabric. Across cultures and timelines, moss has consistently represented endurance, tranquility, and life's persistent march forward.

The echoes of the past still resonate in our modern context, inspiring a renewed appreciation for moss, an entity that challenges our perception of grandeur, compelling us to respect and admire the beauty in the small, the quiet, and the slow. The world of moss, seeping into our cultural narrative quietly yet persistently, serves as a compelling reminder that the smallest things often harbor the most profound wisdom.

Chapter 5. Moss Warriors: Unbelievable Adaptations of Forest Moss

As the sunlight pierces through the emerald canopy, be it a rainforest, boreal, or temperate forest, your eyes may be drawn towards the stately trees, the vivacious canopy, or perhaps even the lively fauna. And while these staples of the forest ecosystem may easily capture your attention, it's worth stooping down, allowing your gaze to meet the quiet, often unnoticed inhabitants of the forest floor—our moss warriors.

5.1. The Basics of Moss

Miniature yet mighty, mosses are humble powerhouses that play fundamental roles in the forest ecosystem. As the premier colonizers of land, about 500 million years ago, they serve as a living testament to the unyielding resilience of life. Comprised of about 22,000 known species across the globe, the unassuming and often overlooked mosses are indeed chameleons of survival, displaying an array of unbelievable adaptations built over eons.

Mosses are non-vascular plants, meaning they lack xylem and phloem—the 'veins' of vascular plants—which are responsible for transporting nutrients and water throughout the plant. This characterization may initially appear as a limiting factor; however, for mosses, this seemingly simple structural makeup facilitates their unique, almost supernatural capacities to survive even in the harshest environments.

5.2. The Many Faces of Moss

Characterized by minute and often inconspicuous leafy structures, a typical moss lifecycle comprises two distinct phases: the gametophyte and the sporophyte stage. In the gametophyte phase, the mature and dominant moss plant produces the sperm and egg cells, ensuing in the formation of the sporophyte (aka the reproduction phase), whereupon the spores are released and hence the circle of life continues.

It may seem a standard plant lifecycle, yet the secret to moss' survival lies tucked away in these seemingly mundane processes. Consider the sporophyte phase, where the spreading of spores is an elegant dance of chance and strategy. The spores, encapsulated in a structure called the sporangium or 'spore capsule,' sit atop the elongated seta, a kind of stalk. Sealed by an operculum, a protective cap, these spores wait for the perfect moment to embark on their journey. The very opening of this cap is a remarkable adaptation in itself—sensitive to the slightest changes in humidity, allowing the precise release of spores during favorable conditions.

5.3. Moss and Water: An Epic Romance

Mosses show a unique affinity towards water, linked to various ecological adaptations they possess. With their non-vascular nature, mosses directly absorb water and nutrients from their surroundings, primarily the immediate environment of rain, dew, or bridal veil-like mist.

This absorption is made possible through tiny, hair-like structures known as rhizoids that anchor the moss to its substrate, often a tree trunk, rock, or the earthly forest floor. Unlike the roots of vascular plants, moss rhizoids don't absorb nutrients; instead, every cell of the moss is capable of absorbing water and nutrients directly. This is a fine example of how mosses turn their potential limitation into a survival advantage.

5.4. Moss Battles: Extreme Territories

Mosses are nature's true warriors—never shying away from extreme confrontations, they are capable of inhabiting a range of environments, from arctic tundras to hot deserts, thanks largely to their brilliant moisture retention capabilities. They can efficiently conserve water during dry periods through various methods, such as curling their tiny leaves inward, reducing their surface area, and thereby limiting water loss to desiccation.

5.5. Eternal Green: The Resurrection Ability

Perhaps the most unbelievable adaptation of mosses is their 'resurrection ability.' Unlike most plants that wither away and die in the absence of water, mosses follow a different strategy—they simply pause their life processes and wait! Dehydrated mosses can lose up to 98% of their cellular water and still bounce back to life once the water is available.

This desiccation tolerance is not merely a miracle of nature but a fascinating feat of evolutionary adaptation involving considerable cellular and metabolic modifications. Such resilience only heightens the stature of moss as a true warrior of nature.

5.6. Moss and Medicine: Healing Touch

Mosses have also adapted remarkably to reward those who interact with them. Certain types are found to have medicinal properties, owing to their antimicrobial substances. Fulfilling the role of natural bandages, cover, and sterilizer during World War One, the Sphagnum mosses absorbed up to three times their own weight and were more absorbent than cotton.

Our exploration of mosses just about scratches the surface of their depth and reign. Armed with their unique adaptations, they provide invaluable insights into overcoming obstacles and adopting resilience. As a silent forest sentinel, the moss, despite its humble size, shoulders the weight of providing stability, and plays an unparalleled role in maintaining the balance and vitality of a forest ecosystem.

Through these captivating mossy moments, we hope to ignite profound respect and recognition towards these miniature champions of resilience. And in the moss-silhouetted undergrowth, remember that there's an entire world of warriors, standing their ground, silently enriching our world, inspiring us in their own quiet, and infinitely resilient, way.

Chapter 6. Mapping the Moss: Geographic Spread and Diversity

Moss, a quiet yet ubiquitous presence in our world's forests, is vastly more diverse and widespread than one might initially perceive. From the tiled roofs of quaint European villages or the rainy forests of the Pacific Northwest, to the humidities of tropical rainforests, the variety of moss species across divergent geographical regions is both vast and impressive in its resilience and ecological diversity.

6.1. Moss Diversity Across Geological Epochs

Tracing the timeline of moss evolution across geological epochs presents a fascinating journey into the simmering heart of prehistoric times. Mosses, belonging to the division Bryophyta, are among the earliest of terrestrial plants, with the first moss-like plants appearing during the Silurian Period over 430 million years ago. Blink, and swiftly travel in time through the Devonian Period—the "Age of Fishes"—where mosses were starting to become well established on land. As primary producers, they played a vital role in driving early terrestrial ecosystem dynamics.

Humanity's perception of moss has evolved over centuries, from indifferent dismissal to appreciating and recognizing its importance in today's world. Over the years, numerous research has discovered about 12,000 to 13,000 species of moss throughout the world, meticulously cataloged in textbooks and preserved in herbaria across the globe.

6.2. Continental Cornucopia: Moss Diversity Across Continents

Taking a continent-wise look at moss species distribution reveals an intriguing panorama of ecological diversity.

In the Americas, the vast expanse of the Appalachian Mountains hosts over 450 species, including the globally endangered Appalachian grimmia (Grimmia laevigata), while the Pacific Northwest rainforests exhibit a grand display of epiphytic mosses like the Oregon beaked moss (Kindbergia oregana).

Change your direction towards the east, and the enchanting lands of Europe present a varied pattern of moss endemism. The Northern Hemisphere's cold biomes, including the tundra and coniferous forests, play host to diverse sphagnum mosses, immortalized in the bogs, marshes, and peatlands.

Crossing the Ural Mountains, we enter Asia, where the mighty Himalayas alone are home to 900+ moss species. Continue this ecological voyage to the Land of the Rising Sun, encountering the endemic Japanese tornado moss (Vortex japonicum) and the revered Suizenji-northern moss (Cratoneuron filicinum).

Africa, in contrast, presents an assorted cross-section of moss life reflective of its dynamic topographies. From the Kobresia myosuroides covering the Ethiopian Highlands to the rich Bryophyte floras found in the Afromontane forests, the continent's moss flora is a rich tapestry waiting to be unraveled.

Australia, a continent par-excellence for its unique biota, stays true to this distinction in its moss demographics too. From the Pilbara region, noting the xerophytic Gymnostomiella vernicosa, to the Dicranoloma billardierei in the temperate rainforests of Tasmania, the land Down Under presents an array of moss wonders.

6.3. Microhabitats: A Closer Look at Diverse Moss Niches

Exploring the diverse niches mosses occupy offers valuable insights into their environmental impacts and adaptations. From rock surfaces and tree trunks to hydrated soils and water bodies, their ability to thrive in varying circumstances underscores their adaptability and ecological significance.

Above all, the intimate connection mosses establish with their environment is reflective of the symbiotic relationship nature holds, the telling of an unbroken narrative that encapsulates the interconnectedness of life on Earth, from the tiniest moss spore to the largest redwood tree.

In the end, it becomes clear: mosses—a diverse, widespread, and resilient group—are the silent yet crucial anchorage points around which our ecosystems revolve. As the world grapples with the throes of climate change and a biodiversity crisis, understanding these minute giants of the plant kingdom may just open up newer ecological insights. As much as they speak of the world's evolutionary legacy, they whisper prophecies of the future. To pay heed to these whispers, continuing our in-depth exploration of these exquisite beings is quintessential.

In the following chapters, we delve deeper into the microscopic realm of moss, their incredible adaptations, and ecological roles, shaping a mosaic of understanding about these often overlooked but intricately essential components of our natural world. Adventure awaits those willing to tread the moss-freckled path, a journey filled with revelations and marvel, as we continue to delve deeper into the verdant world of moss.

Evidently, mapping the moss proves more than an academic endeavor; it is an exploration into an intricate ecological network, a testament to biodiversity, and a statement about our world's resilience. The geographic spread and diversity of moss is a saga of survival, adaptability, and silent power, waiting to be narrated and keenly listened to.

Chapter 7. The Symbiotic Symphony: Moss and Its Ecosystem

As one steps into the heart of the forest, the soft, damp carpet underfoot is a familiar comfort. This verdant layer, often ignored beneath our very feet, is a thriving ecosystem that sustains the life above and around it. Our protagonist, for this narrative journey, is none other than the modest moss—an unassuming yet vital component of many forest ecosystems.

7.1. The World Beneath Our Feet: What is Moss?

Moss belongs to the division Bryophyta, a group of non-vascular land plants distinctively primitive compared to their vascular relatives, such as ferns, trees, and flowers. They lack roots, flowers, and seeds, and reproduce via spores. Moss plants are small and typically form dense green mats or clumps in damp or shady locations.

While life as a tiny moss might seem mundane to the uninitiated, a closer look reveals a complex and interconnected existence. A colony of moss plants displays a broad range of survival strategies. From reproduction to photosynthesis, these small plants have evolved to harness their circumstance and allow not only their survival but also a symbiotic relationship with their environment.

7.2. The Moss Lifecycle: An Epic Miniature Journey

The lifecycle of a moss plant is a prolonged interplay between two forms: the gametophyte and the sporophyte. During the gametophyte stage, the moss exists as a leafy-green plant, producing male and female structures called gametangia. Water drops—a gift from a rainy day or simply the moisture-laden air—are vital in the transport of male cells to fertilize the female cells, encapsulated within an archegonium.

Once fertilized, these cells produce a sporophyte: a spore-producing structure showing little resemblance to the parent plant. Sporophytes produce a multitude of spores, which are then wind-carried to new locations. Upon making landfall, these spores spawn fresh individual moss plants, thus completing a life cycle intricate yet overlooked.

7.3. The Forest's Little Solar Panels

Though they may be small and unimposing, moss plants are built for survival and function as essential solar energy collectors. The leaves of a moss plant, often just a single cell layer thick, are built for maximum sunlight absorption—an asset vital in a shady forest floor.

The pre-absorbed solar energy powers photosynthesis, the process of converting sunlight into chemical energy—an energy that feeds not only the moss itself but also the network of life surrounding it. Dead and decaying moss feeds fungi and helps grow fresh moss, creating a perpetual cycle of life and contributing to the forest's energy circulation.

7.4. Moss's Role as Nature's Sponge

Moss also possesses nature's most efficient sponges. They can absorb up to twenty times their weight in water, playing a significant role in controlling the ecosystem's water supply. The water-soaked moss releases the moisture slowly, maintaining habitats' humidity levels, preventing soil erosion, and mitigating flood risks.

Moreover, these water banks do not just store rainwater but also capture water from mist and fog, channeling it into the forest floor. Moss, hence, serves as a lifeline, acting as an intermediary in the water cycle, ensuring the entire ecosystem keeps thriving.

7.5. Symbiotic Relationships: Moss and Other Flora and Fauna

Mosses' ability to prosper in a variety of ecological niches has allowed them to form numerous symbiotic relationships within their environment. They provide a habitat for a plethora of insects and microorganisms, serve as a protective layer for tree seeds to sprout, and help orchids and other epiphytes to latch onto and grow.

The inconspicuous moss serves as the bed for trees to take root and a nursery for seedlings. This symbiotic relationship is vital, enhancing forest diversity and contributing significantly to the survival and growth of different plant species.

7.6. Final Notes: Moss, an Ecosystem's Unsung Hero

In summary, mosses are vital components of forest ecosystems. As environmental buffers, water reservoirs, and energy producers, moss's unique biology contributes to the overall health, biodiversity, and resilience of the ecosystems they inhabit—a symphony of interdependencies. Their survival strategies reflect thousands of years of evolutionary adaptation, testament to nature's astoundingly creative resilience, and a testament to their persistence in the face of adversity.

Mosses remind us that every organism, no matter how small, plays a role in the harmony of an ecosystem. As we continue to unveil the mysteries of these diminutive powerhouses, we reiterate the importance of conservation and sustainability. Only by preserving their habitats can we completely appreciate and take advantage of the fascinating world of mosses and the forests they inhabit.

This chapter has given you a glimpse beneath the tree canopy and into the delicate world underfoot. We turn our gaze next to another fascinating component of forest ecosystems. Watch for the upcoming chapter where we unravel the fascinating world of tree fungi and their symbiotic relationships deep within the heart of the forest.

Chapter 8. Sustainability Champions: Moss in Climate Regulation

Imagine embarking on a tour through a dew spangled woodland, the air thick with a damp, rich scent that clings to every moss-covered stone and fills your senses. As you make your way down playful trails of ferns honoring the coolness of the morning, it may be easy to overlook the abundance of the moss. This lush, velvet-like mat, so commonly perceived as 'just background', plays a pivotal role in maintaining the climate balance of our planet. Often underestimated in their ecological significance, mosses are the unsung heroes in climate regulation. It's time we turn the spotlight on these marvels of the botanical world.

8.1. The Moss: A Miniature Forest Dwellers

Mosses are non-vascular plants that belong to the taxonomic division Bryophyta. Short in stature but colossal in contribution, they lend a beautiful green cover serving as a verdant carpet to the forest floor. These miniature forest dwellers bind soil together, acting as erosion control agents while conserving water and providing shelter and food to numerous invertebrates and microorganisms.

8.2. How Does Moss Contribute to Climate Regulation?

Moss assumes a crucial role in the carbon cycle, a fundamental biochemical process basic to the existence and preservation of life on Earth. Terrestrial mosses are capable of absorbing enormous amounts of carbon dioxide, the surplus of which in the atmosphere triggers global warming. They act as excellent sinks of carbon, sequestering it from the atmosphere and consequently decelerating intensifying climate anomalies.

Type of Moss	Role in Climate Regulation	Region
Sphagnum	Integral to peatland ecosystems, known for exceptional carbon storage capabilities	Temperate, Alpine, Arctic, parts of the Tropic
Polytrichum	Frequently thrive in disturbed or poor-quality soil and help in carbon sequestration	Global distribution
Leucobryum	Can withstand dry conditions; sequesters carbon during moisture availability	Global distribution

8.3. Sphagnum: The Super Moss

Sphagnum or peat moss is particularly potent at climate regulation. As these plants die, they decompose to create layers of acidic peat. The carbon captured during their lifetime gets locked away in these peatland ecosystems. The sheer abundance of sphagnum moss in bogs and peatlands contributes to an atmospheric carbon reduction remarkably, with peatlands alone storing roughly one-third of the world's total soil carbon.

8.4. Moss and Nitrogen Fixation

Mosses provide other benefits, such as nitrogen fixation. They work with symbiotic cyanobacteria, which convert atmospheric nitrogen into usable forms, essential for plant growth. This process of nitrogen fixation reduces the carbon barrier and further fortifies sequestering soil carbon, emphasizing moss's invaluable contribution to climate regulation.

8.5. Moss, a Bioindicator of Climate Change

Mosses are highly sensitive to their environmental conditions. A change in the moss population or state can indicate changes to local climate conditions. Mosses aren't just sustaining our climate but also informing us about the changes we need to pay attention to, thus playing the role of climate change's silent sentinels.

8.6. Efforts for Preservation: A Race against Time

Human-driven changes, such as deforestation, wildfires, and land development, are endangering moss and their habitats. As we lose moss, we are also losing an important ally in our battle against climate change. Therefore, globally concerted efforts are imperative to protect these potent climate regulation agents.

8.7. Conservation and Public Partnership

In recognizing this threat, many conservation campaigns now enlist the public's help in documenting and protecting moss. Citizen-science projects, such as the British Bryological Society's "Sphagnum Hunt," encourage eco-conscious individuals to help safeguard these unsung heroes of the natural world.

8.8. Science and Technology on Moss Side

Meanwhile, in the scientific community, the emphasis is on studying mosses' potential role in carbon sequestration. Combining climate models with advances in plant physiology research can enhance our understanding of mosses' role in climate regulation. Innovative moss-restoration techniques are also being developed to recover degraded peatlands.

8.9. The Way Forward

Protection and conservation of mosses—our natural climate regulators—is no longer a choice but an absolute necessity. Our survival relies on safeguarding these little green warriors who, quietly and unassumingly, work tirelessly towards maintaining the fine ecological balance. The more we learn about them, the better equipped we'll be to ensure their survival – and ours. Thus, renewing our commitment to these guardians of the earth and dedicating ourselves to sustainable practices encompassing these humble life forms becomes our shared responsibility. Let's continue to honor and protect these sustainability champions of the botanical realm.

Through 'Moss Moments: Exploring the World's Most Enchanting Forests', we hope to inspire a newfound appreciation for these climate regulators and our shared journey towards a resilient and sustainable future. Like moss, let's grow together towards that goal.

Chapter 9. Tiny Architects: Moss Structures and their Fascinations

As feather-light spores alight on damp forest floors, nascent moss colonies take shape, their initial templates woven in the intimate embrace of patience, time, and elemental talent. Over the course of their existence, mosses become architectonic masterpieces—tiny assemblages of plants, often overlooked, yet bristling with verdant complexity.

Round upon round of humble fronds splay out across the woodland floor or climb tree trunks, their ample intricacies a testament to their persistent struggle and triumphant adaptation to withstand nature's tempestuous conditions.

9.1. The Marvel of Moss Morphology

Each moss-tiniest structure, renowned as a gametophyte, is a composite of fastidious design. Their stems rise upward from the substratum, bearing leaves typically just a cell-layer thick. Each leaf, small though it may be, channels a labyrinth of cells designed to capture and retain moisture.

The leaves, while simple in form, are vastly diverse in structure, presenting themselves with pointed or rounded tips, toothed or smooth edges, and an array of specialized cells for photosynthesis and water retention. Their grooved midribs, known as 'costa', direct the surface runoff, the lifeblood of a moss, deep within the plant's structure where it is stored and tactfully utilized.

Such multifaceted morphology—the compact shape, the spiraling leaf arrangement, the alluring green hue—has refined itself over countless millennia, optimizing the moss's survival and success in the least conducive conditions.

9.2. The Sporophyte: A Dance of Life and Death

Once a moss has matured, part of it undergoes transformation to form a sporophyte. This shift builds a new, orthogonal plant that shoots up from the arcane web of green, often possessing a remarkably different form, wearing a hue of brown or lofty red. The sporophyte, containing the capsule crowned by a peristome, serves as a secure safehouse for its soon-to-be-launched spores.

The spore is arguably the most defiant and adventurous part of the life cycle of moss. Born in the guarded protection of the sporophytes, it eventually sets off on a solitary expedition and either finds refuge amidst challenging conditions or succumbs to them. This life-cycle, cyclical as it is, pits the humility of the gametophyte against the audacity of the sporophyte—an elegant ballet of survival and nature's essential pulse.

9.3. Moss Colonies: The Forest's Unsung Heroes

Moss colonies develop over extended periods—uncounted decades or even centuries, weaving a living cloak over a forest's rough skin. By incessantly trapping moisture, mosses provide a crucial lifeline for other forest inhabitants such as lichens, liverworts, and innumerable tiny life forms, thus playing a pivotal role in preserving biodiversity.

These tiny architects also contribute to the slow, inexorable process of soil creation, breaking down stones, capturing organic matter, and sustaining miniature water cycles within their structure. Their active role in tackling climate change is increasingly recognized, as peat mosses lock significant amounts of carbon within their layers, quietly and persistently working to take care of the planet's health.

9.4. Peering into a Moss City: The Microcosm within

Mosses also house a labyrinthine microcosm within their fronds—a world thriving with microbial life. Water-filled interstitial spaces within the moss structure serve as aquatic habitats for microscopic aquatic creatures like rotifers, tardigrades, and nematodes, along with countless species of bacteria and fungi.

These microorganisms enter a realm of vertical jungles where climbing a single stalk of moss would be akin to scaling a towering sequoia. This biosphere within a biosphere forms a complex web of life and death, an intricately balanced ecological network.

9.5. The Magic of Bryology: The Study of Mosses

To fully appreciate the wonders of moss, one may delve into Bryology—the scientific study of these admirable organisms. From close examination of moss species under the microscope, taxonomical identification, to exploring mosses' role in ecological functions or understanding their physiology at a molecular level, Bryology illuminates the moss world for the curious mind.

Bryologists endeavor to elucidate the ecology, evolution, and manifold utilities of mosses, rallying the knowledge of these fascinating green pioneers into a concerted effort to preserve, protect, and promote our forests.

In conclusion, the moss-covered forest floors, the moss-clad tree trunks, or the mossy traces on a disregarded rock embody encapsulated time capsules of plant evolution—a testament to nature's resilience savvied through their tiny, embellished structures. They instruct us, in their soft-spoken-wise way, about the interconnections of our ecosystems, silently urging us to play our part in preserving and respecting the delicate harmony of our shared home, the Earth.

Dive into your local woods to experience these wonders, or continue turning pages with us, as the next chapter will lead us further down into this enchanted, mossy realm.

Chapter 10. Humans and Moss: Historical Uses and Modern Applications

Moss: No ordinary plant, but a botanic wonder that has played an intricate role in human history. In our modern world, it continues to stretch its reach to various sectors, redefining our connection with nature.

10.1. From the Stone Age to the Age of Sail

In the tender beginnings of human civilization, across icy landscapes where resources were scarce, moss was more than just a plant—it was saviour. Our ancient ancestors harvested peat moss to fuel their hearths. The camphor-like scent was more than an atmospheric element within their dwellings; it, in fact, acted as a repellent against insects. Meanwhile, the heat provided a crucial lifeline in hostile climates, essential in maintaining manageable living conditions.

Navigating further through our shared history, moss had a pivotal maritime role, especially during the Age of Sail. With no access to fresh produce during long voyages, sailors succumbed to the harrowing disease of scurvy. Here, the saga of moss takes an unexpected turn to heroism. Vitamin C-rich species like **Sphagnum** were consumed by sailors to prevent the disease. A striking illustration of the botanical world's indispensable role in shaping human history.

10.2. In the War Trenches

Not only has moss been a co-pilot during maritime explorations, but it has also been a companion in the trenches of world wars. Common moss species like **Sphagnum** found utilization as wound dressings for their absorbent properties, staving off antiseptic shortage during the WWI. Legend says these make-shift bandages, dubbed as 'Sphagnum moss bandages', played a decisive role in rescuing hundreds of lives by not only staunching blood flow but also reducing infections, thanks to the plant's inherent antiseptic properties.

10.3. Moss in Architecture and Urban Life

In our urban habitats, moss has found a permanent place by adding green shades to our grey lives. Roofing, popularly known as 'moss roofing', uses dried moss to fill gaps between roofing tiles, providing insulation and preventing rain seepage.

Not just roofs, moss walls, or 'green walls' is another captivating application. City dwellers are using moss to create living artwork, both inside and outside their homes. It's a style statement and a step towards embracing the green lifestyle.

10.4. Moss and the Lens

Moss has been a muse for artists, poets, photographers, and cinematographers alike. From crafting mesmerizing miniature worlds for photography to creating unique immersive experiences for audiences in films—the role of moss has been prominent, yet often unnoticed.

10.5. Pioneering Eco-sustainability

Today, the value and applicability of moss have extended beyond aesthetics and stepped into the realm of environmental science. Pioneers harness its potential to create sustainable, innovative solutions to environmental issues. The plant's ability to absorb heavy metals from polluted environments brings fresh hope for eco-restoration.

Global efforts are underway to use moss to absorb city pollutants effectively. The initiative, often referred to as 'Green City Solutions', focuses on reducing the urban CO_2 footprint.

10.6. Medical Frontiers

On the medical frontier, researchers are delving into moss's medicinal properties to improve healthcare. With its inherent antiseptic qualities, scientists open new avenues for advancements in medical treatments. As we continue to discover more about this delicate plant, its myriad potential in improving lives and conserving our world continues to unfurl.

10.7. Conclusion: Moss in Our Daily Lives

A single narrative cannot encapsulate the myriad roles moss has played and continues to play in our lives. It's a tale that transcends traditional botanic companionship. The journey of moss is, thus, intertwined with our own journey, from early beginnings to the present, and probably into the future. As we write new chapters of innovation, conservation, and exploration, moss, in its different shades and forms, will always be a part of our narrative, etching its vital mark in every sphere of human life.

In an era seeking sustainability, the unfolding story of moss is a testimony to the fact that solutions to our pressing problems may well lie in embracing the wisdom inherent in nature. It's a relationship we have nurtured for centuries, and one set to deepen as we unlock the full potential of moss in our lives.

Chapter 11. Safeguarding the Green: Conservation and You

In the heart of nature's grand tapestry lies the mossy woods—a sanctuary for myriad species and a testament to the earth's inherent resilience. Just as these enchanting habitats foster biodiversity and nurture life, they invite us to reciprocate through thoughtful, dedicated, and informed conservation efforts. Unfolding within these verdant canopies are stories that underscore the critical roles we can play in preserving and protecting these natural havens.

11.1. Green Footprints: Our Significance in Conservation

Stepping into the realm of forest conservation, one can't underestimate the power that individual initiatives carry. It is not just large organizations or governments that bear the responsibility of conserving natural resources. You, the individual, have a significant role to play as well.

Forest conservation, at its core, is about symbiotic relationships—between the flora, the fauna, and us humans. By minimizing our ecological footprints, we can contribute remarkably to maintaining the health and vivacity of these ecosystems. We start this journey by recognizing our direct and indirect interactions with the environment, understanding the effects of our actions, and making environmentally conscious choices about resource consumption.

11.2. Small Steps, Big Changes

Little drops of water make a mighty ocean, and likewise, small conservation efforts accumulate to effect substantial change. Recall how simply reducing paper usage had a profound impact on pulp industries and subsequently, on deforestation rates? Similarly, intentional actions such as reducing waste, recycling, adopting sustainable materials, or consciously opting for greener alternatives in our daily lives contributes considerably to safeguarding our forests. It doesn't stop there. As we promote and embody these practices, we inspire those around us to do the same, fostering an extended community of conservationists.

11.3. Understanding Endemics: The Need for Regional Efforts

While a broad, holistic approach to conservation is valuable, it's equally important to understand regional specifics. Each forest ecosystem is characterized by unique sets of flora and fauna—species that are endemic and provide diverse ecological services. By engaging in local conservation efforts, we can help preserve these critical and unique biodiversity hotspots.

11.4. Sustainable Tourism: Embracing Responsibility

Another aspect of our interaction with forests takes the form of tourism. There's a fine line between enjoying these natural wonders and inadvertently contributing to their degradation. By focusing on sustainable tourism—maintaining low visitor impact, promoting environmental awareness, and providing beneficial experiences for both visitors and hosts—we can tread this line wisely. Practicing 'leave no trace' ethics, we contribute our part in making tourism a sustainable allied industry to conservation.

11.5. Involved Conservation: Citizen Science and You

Citizen science is a wonderful opportunity to jump-start your conservation journey and involves public participation and collaboration in scientific research. Whether it's participating in bird counts, logging nature observations, or contributing essential data for wildlife research, readily accessible applications make it feasible to get involved, regardless of where you reside.

11.6. Legislating Preservation: Your Role in Policy

Policy-making can sound daunting, but the individual's role here remains potent. Write to your local representatives about conservation you care about, attend public discussion forums, and vote for legislation and candidates supportive of environmental preservation. By doing this, you contribute to a legislative environment that aids and encourages forest conservation, a step closer to a greener planet.

11.7. Community Ventures: Nurture Your Neighborhood

Getting involved in local communities that foster nature conservation, engage in clean-up drives, plant trees and remove invasive species, can be a rewarding and impactful experience. Empowered communities play crucial roles in forest conservation, especially in safeguarding smaller, community-owned forest patches. Your engagement can be a catalyst for larger community action.

In the end, the intricate tapestry of conservation is woven from various strands—ecological understanding, individual efforts, sustainable choices, and community engagement. As we tread softly amidst the green, let us remember that every footprint counts. We are all part layers of this tapestry, impacting and being impacted by, the mossy woods and their inhabitants. Deep within these green wonderlands, we not only discover life in its myriad forms but also recognize our own roles in safeguarding it. Let the journey of discovering the green and safeguarding it with fervour and understanding, begin today.

www.ingramcontent.com/pod-product-compliance
Lightning Source LLC
Chambersburg PA
CBHW062308290526
45794CB00006B/2729